FLORIDA ESTATE PLAN

JUST THE BASICS

First Edition

By Gadiel A. Espinoza, MBA, JD

Foreword by Michelle E. Espinoza, CPA, MAcc

LEGAL JARGON :)

DEDICATION STATEMENT

To my mother and father, Ruth and Guillermo Espinoza, who came to this country with nothing but a dream. A dream that they would live a better life. A life where their children would have the opportunity of publishing a book.

To my wife, Michelle. The one who has been such an inspiration to me. The one who has inspired me to become the best version of myself.

To my kids, Liam and Lucas. The reasons I get up in the morning and do what I do. And the reason I look forward to coming home every day.

CONTENTS

FOREWORD vii

ACKNOWLEDGEMENTS ix

INTRODUCTION xi

1—THE ESTATE 1

    Estate 1

    Estate Plan 1

    Estate Plan Purpose 1

    Estate Plan Team 2

    Objectives 3

2—NET WORTH 5

    Estate Value 5

    Debt Worth 5

    Net Worth 5

3—THE BLUEPRINT 7

    Getting Started 7

    Last Will and Testament 7

4—FLORIDA LAWS 9

    Divorce 9

    Abatement 9

    Ademption 10

    Antilapse 10

    Intestate 10

    Children 11

5—OTHER STRATEGIES 13

    Other Strategies 13

    Payable on Death Accounts 13

    Transfer on Death Accounts 13

    Tenancy by the Entirety Bank Accounts 14

Joint Tenancy with Right of Survivorship...14
Life Estate Deed...14

6—THE LIVING TRUST 15

Living Trust...15
Benefits of a Trust..15

7—UNCLE SAM 17

Florida Taxes..17
Federal Taxes 17
Tax Act..17

8—OTHER DOCS...19

Power of Attorney...19
Health Care Surrogate Designation...19
Living Will 20
Preneed Guardian Designation 20
Final Arrangements...20
Letter of Intent 21

9—THE KIDS...23

Create the Plan...23
Kids' Trust...23
Guardian 23
Designation of a Health Care Surrogate of a Minor.........................23
Uniform Transfers to Minors Act 24

10—PROBATE...25

Probate...25
Cost of Probate..25

11—THE VIEW FROM ABOVE..27

Why do any of this?..27

CONCLUSION..29

ABOUT THE AUTHOR 31

FOREWORD

This book was written in a manner that would allow anyone who has never done any kind of estate planning or gone through a probate proceeding, to simply pick up this book and obtain a general, but good understanding of the subject matter. Gadiel does an excellent job taking a hard to understand subject matter, and turning it into something that is easy to comprehend. Plus, he is my hubby, and I love him so much! Enjoy!

by Michelle E. Espinoza, CPA MAcc

ACKNOWLEDGEMENTS

I would like to start by thanking the many people who have helped shape me into the 'me' I am today, but for that I would need to write another book, so I will simply make a short list. First, and foremost, I thank God for everything. God has blessed me with so much that words alone cannot adequately describe what God has done for me. Second, I thank my mother, *Mami*, and my father, *Viejo*. For loving me! For always believing in me, even when everyone, including myself did not believe in me. I love you! I owe everything to you! I thank my wonderful wife, Michelle. God knew what I needed in my life. I went from being in the arms of my mother to the one who would inspire me to become what I should be. I love you so much! Lastly, to my kids, Liam Joseph and Lucas Peyton. I love you guys with all of my heart. You guys are the reason for believing.

INTRODUCTION

In my experience, most people looking into estate planning do so because there was some crisis in their family, which means that they are most likely too late in doing anything preventative to avoid Probate and Guardianship Court. However, if you are reading this book and you have not had a crisis in your family, you are probably in good hands. So, enjoy reading this book, as much as I enjoyed writing it.

1

THE ESTATE

Estate. An estate is everything you own at the time of your death! It is that simple. So, this means your clothes, household furniture, Christmas tree, jewelry, shoes, gun collection, bookcase filled with tons of books (including this book), car, red corvette, primary residence, vacation home in Miami, rental property in Orlando, checking account, savings account, cd account, 403b, 401k, IRA, art collection, coin collection, antiques, business, life insurance policy, motorcycle, bicycle, moped, boat, kayak, and even your family dog and cat are included in your estate. It is literally everything you own, whether tangible or intangible, becomes part of your estate. And after you pass away, your property must be transferred to its new owners whom are your heirs, also known as your beneficiaries. Oh! Do not forget about your digital assets. i.e., Facebook, Instagram, Twitter, blogs, websites, photos, and Bitcoins, etc. All of this is also part of your estate.

Estate Plan. An estate plan is the process of planning what you want to do with your property upon your death using a written plan, whether it is a Last Will and Testament, Living Trust, or some other document.

Estate Plan Purpose. There are several reasons why you should create an estate plan.

1. To ensure your property goes to those who you choose;
2. To prevent and/or minimize the court's ability to interfere;
3. To minimize the amount Uncle Sam takes from your estate;

4. To ease the transferring process of your property on your family, and not leave them with the headaches of not knowing what you would have wanted to do with your property, which often leaves them fighting amongst themselves because you failed to plan; and

5. To be in total control of your property upon your death, not the State of Florida, opportunistic family members, estranged child, enemies, ex-spouse(s), or neighbor, etc.

Estate Plan Team. Below are the people who will play an important role in your estate planning.

1. **Your Attorney**. He or she is the most important person on your team. Your attorney will be the one providing you advice on everything, every step of the way. If you do not have an attorney, you can either ask a close friend or relative for a referral, or simply conduct a Google search in your local area. If you go with Google, make sure to read the attorney's reviews before scheduling an initial consultation. Thereafter, the attorney will pretty much take care of the entire process. At your initial consultation, expect to have a discussion with the attorney about your assets, family, and goals. Ultimately, they will ask you, what are your objectives in regard to your property. That is, *What do you want to do with your property?* The attorney will then discuss how your objectives can be accomplished. E.g., Transferring property using a Last Will and Testament, Living Trust, Quit Claim Deed, etc.

2. **Your Tax Preparer**. Your attorney will be in contact with your Tax Preparer in order to work together for a common goal. i.e., Use the best estate planning strategies to minimize how you much you will pay to Uncle Sam.

3. **Your Financial Planner**. Your financial planner will be a part of your estate planning, if you have significant size retirement accounts.

4. **Your Insurance Agent.** Your insurance agent is the one who has either sold you a home or life insurance policy or some other product, such as disability insurance.

These individuals will work together to complete your estate plan. However, your attorney is the one executing the plays. Imagine yourself as the coach of a basketball team, and your attorney, tax preparer, financial planner, and insurance agent are the players. The star player is your attorney. Your attorney is like your Kobe Bryant. The all-star on your team. He is the one who receives the plays from you, but the attorney while leading the others will execute the plays.

Objectives. Your objectives are simply what you want to do with your property. Who gets your property, in which order, and when. The main thing to keep in mind is that your objectives are your desires and your estate planning documents that are drafted by your attorney will describe those desires.

2

NET WORTH

Estate Value. As mentioned in Chapter 1, everything you own is part of your estate, which includes your debt. Moreover, in order to determine the value of your estate, you will only include property that has value. But how do you determine the value of your personal property? Well, if you recently purchased some of your things, you could simply search on the interweb and see what they are selling for. You could search on eBay, Amazon, and Google, etc. Things such as jewelry and furniture can be appraised by a professional. Your home, however, will need to be apprised unless it was recently purchased. If you do not want to spend the money on an appraiser, you could simply go on Zillow.com and see what the comparable homes in your area are selling for. It's that simple!

Debt Worth. So, once you have determined the value of your assets, you must subtract the associated debt. i.e., If your home has a loan, subtract the loan amount from the home.

Net Worth. Once you subtract all your debt from your assets, you will have your net worth. Hopefully, the number is positive! :) That should be the goal at least.

3

THE BLUEPRINT

Getting Started. Once you have determined the value of your estate, your attorney will assist you in completing the Estate Plan Intake form, which will include all of your assets. Another important aspect of estate planning is to list the beneficiaries next to the assets. For example, if you have several bank accounts, you will list the beneficiaries or the joint account owners (if applicable) next to the respective bank accounts. This will let you and your attorney whether you have beneficiaries or joint account owners listed, which means that if you die, the aforementioned accounts may or may not need to be probated in order for the money to transfer to the new owner. *More on Probate later.* However, if you know that you are aware of what could happen, you have the option of adding someone as a beneficiary, so that they can receive the funds upon your passing without going through the trouble and headache of probate. Once you have completed the Estate Plan Intake form, you can now discuss your goals and objectives, and how each estate planning document can help you reach them.

Last Will and Testament. A Last Will & Testament is a document that provides instructions on how your property will be distributed at the time of your death. It allows you to dictate who gets your property at the time of your death, instead of the courts deciding for you. In your will you may name a personal representative (executor) who will be responsible for managing your estate. This person may be a family member or friend, bank or trust company. You can even name a guardian to care for your minor children and their property in your will, or establish a trust. You can also disinherit someone. However, the main drawback of using a will is that it does not avoid probate.

4

FLORIDA LAWS

Divorce. Florida law states that if you get divorced, have your marriage annulled, or dissolved, any and all clauses in your will that speak about your ex-spouse will automatically be revoked, as if they were not even mentioned in your will to begin with. This means your ex-spouse receives nothing from your estate, unless you amend your will or draft a new will and specifically add them again. This benefits many recently divorcees because many do not update their will upon finalizing their divorce. It's truly an afterthought. It's not until someone dies or gets remarried that they think about revisiting their will. The Florida legislators created this law to protect heirs from essentially being disinherited after a divorce. So, it goes without saying that it is very important to update your will as soon as there is a significant change in your circumstance, such as a divorce, or death.

Abatement. Florida law states that if you do not have enough assets at the time of your death, this law will come into play, and rectify the issue. For example, if you have $25,000.00 of credit card bills upon your death, but you stated in your will that your son will receive $35,000.00, unfortunately, your son will not receive $35,000.00. He will only receive $10,000.00, and this is assuming that there is money to pay for the attorney's fees and costs of administering the estate. You see, the estate's debts must be paid off before anyone receives a penny. So, if you planned on passing away with a whole lot of debt with the idea of leaving some money to your heirs, think again. This is one of the main reasons why it is extremely important to have a game plan. i.e., a good estate plan. This is one of the things that you will be discussing with your attorney as you draft the estate plan.

Ademption. Florida law states that if you leave a gift to someone in your will that you don't have at the time of your death, the intended beneficiary simply does not receive that gift. However, just like many laws, this one has an exception. If the intended gift was sold, the beneficiary may be entitled to the proceeds of the sale of that gift. But, often if you do not have the gift because you gave it away, lost it, sold it, or whatever the case may be, this law will dictate how to handle the specific situation.

Antilapse. Florida law states that if your beneficiary passes away before you do, their gift will pass to their living heirs. For example, if you left your daughter your red 1994 Pontiac Sunbird in your will, but she passed away before you did and you never changed your will, her living heirs would inherit the Sunbird. This is because Florida has the enacted the Antilapse statute. On the other hand, if that was not your intended objective, it is important to have contingent beneficiaries listed in your will.

Intestate. Florida law states that if you die without having executed a will, the intestate succession law will dictate who gets your property through the probate process. However, only the property that's titled solely in your name will be probated. Under the intestate succession statute, the property to be distributed depends on who's alive in your family. Below is a breakdown on who gets what and how much.

If you die:	Who gets what:
• With children, but no spouse.	• children receives 100%
• With a spouse, but no descendants.	• spouse receives 100%
• With a spouse and descendants from you and that spouse, and the spouse has no other descendants	• spouse receives 100%
• With a spouse and descendants from you and that spouse, and the spouse has descendants from another relationship.	• spouse receives 50% of your intestate property • your descendants receives 50% of your intestate property
• With a spouse and descendants from you and someone other than that spouse.	• spouse receives 50% of your intestate property • your descendants receives 50% of your intestate property
• With parents, but no spouse or descendants.	• parents receive 100%
• With siblings, but no spouse, descendants, or parents.	• siblings inherit 100%

Children. In order for your children to receive any of your property under the intestate succession statute, they must be legally recognized as your children. Obviously, your biological children qualify as your legal children, along with children who you have legally adopted. However, foster children and stepchildren that you have not legally adopted are not legally recognized as your children, thus they will not receive your property under the intestate succession statute. Moreover, children that you have placed for adoption and were subsequently adopted by another family will not receive your property. On the contrary, children conceived by you but born after your death will still receive their respective share of your property. Lastly, children born outside of a marriage will be able to receive their respective share of your property if you were married, but it turned out to be void; a court determines your paternity before or after your death; or you execute a document acknowledging your paternity.

5

OTHER STRATEGIES

Other Strategies. Will substitutions are alternatives to wills, and sometimes it is the better option. For example, Joint Tenancy Bank Accounts, holding property by Tenancy by the Entirety, Payable-on-death Accounts, and Life Estate Deeds are all will substitutions, which means that they go outside of the will. In other words, if you use any of these estate planning strategies to transfer your assets upon your death, it will not be necessary nor does it carry any validity if they are stated in your will, and will avoid probate.

Payable on Death Accounts. Florida law allows this type of bank account (known as a Totten Trust or Poor Man's Trust) that will pass to your named beneficiary upon your death, which allows them to avoid probate. i.e., the court process of transferring your assets to your heirs upon your death. Setting up the account is very simple. When you open up the account, or at some later date upon opening it, you designate a beneficiary to receive the funds when you die. Remember, a beneficiary is not a joint account holder, but simply the person to receive what's left in the account when you pass away. However, if there is a joint account holder listed, this person has right to the funds primarily. So, if they withdraw all of the funds and close the account, there is nothing for the beneficiary to inherit.

Transfer on Death Accounts. Florida law allows this type of account, which also avoids probate. Florida allows people who own stocks and bonds to designate beneficiaries by registering the accounts in transfer-on-death forms. Upon your passing, your beneficiary will automatically inherit the account without having to deal with probate. The beneficiary will communicate directly with the financial institution.

Tenancy by the Entirety Bank Accounts. Florida law states that if you establish a bank account as a tenancy by the entirety account, one spouse does not have the authority on their own to transfer funds from the account without the expressed consent of the other account holder. It's really that simple. So, be mindful on how you open the bank account. Make sure you read and check the appropriate box. Ask questions if you have any doubts.

Joint Tenancy with Right of Survivorship. Florida law states that if you establish a bank account as joint tenancy with right of survivorship, either joint account holder can transfer funds out, and a joint owner's withdrawal of funds from a joint bank account terminates the joint tenancy nature of the funds and severs the right of survivorship as to the funds withdrawn. In other words, as far as the withdrawn funds are concerned, the other joint owner does not have the survivorship right to those funds, if the person who withdrew the funds passes away.

Life Estate Deed. Florida law allows this special type of deed to be used in order to avoid probate. It is a type of ownership of real property that allows the property owner an interest in the property during their lifetime, and upon their death, that interest is then transferred to the listed beneficiary on the deed. This transfer is no different than your bank transferring your funds from your checking account to your designated beneficiary upon your death.

6

THE LIVING TRUST

Living Trust. Florida law allows property to be transferred via a living trust. A living trust is similar to a will in that it is used to transfer property to beneficiaries upon the death of the original property owner. However, the key difference between the two estate planning documents is that a living trust allows you to control the property while alive, and avoids probate, which is why it is called a 'living' trust. The transfer occurs while you are alive, however, the beneficiary does not receive the property until after you die. Creating the trust is similar to preparing a will. Your attorney will gather some basic information from you. i.e., Information about you, your family, and your assets. Once completed, your attorney will ask you about your desires for each piece of property to determine if a living trust is the right estate planning document for you. In general, your residential home will be your biggest asset, unless you have investment properties. Once you have determined which property will be transferred into the trust, and the trust is created, you now must "fund" the trust, which means you must transfer your assets into the trust. For example, if you are to transfer your primary residence into your trust, you must execute a quitclaim deed naming the trustee as the new grantee. If your assets are not properly transferred (funded) into your trust, they will not be a part of the trust, and will become part of your probatable estate, which essentially defeats the purpose of creating the trust in the first place.

Benefits of a Trust. As previously mentioned, a trust will avoid probate because you are no longer the owner, because the trustee is the new owner. Probatable assets are the ones titled solely in the decedent's name, but if the assets are titled in the trustee's name, it's no longer titled in the decedent's name, hence, not probatable assets. Another benefit of using a living trust is that it provides you control of your property even if you were to lose capacity or die. The trust property is now controlled by your Successor Trustee, which is the trustee you appointed to take your place upon your incapacitation or death.

7

UNCLE SAM

Florida Taxes. When it comes to estate planning, taxes is perhaps the most complicated areas to deal with. Fortunately, Florida does not impose an estate, gift or inheritance tax.

Federal Taxes. The yearly exclusion from gift tax is $15,000.00, which means that you could give a gift of no more than $15,000.00 to a person each year without tapping into your gift tax exemption in 2019. Of course, this amount is adjusted every year for inflation to the nearest $1,000.00. This represents a great tax strategy to use in order to give away assets without tax liability each year. You do not want to miss out on the opportunity of avoiding transfer taxes.

Tax Act. A lot has changed to the Tax Cuts and Jobs Act, also known as the Tax Act. The federal estate and gift tax exemption, specifically, the amount you can give away without being liable to paying taxes is $11.4 million (minus prior taxable gifts) in 2019, which means married couples can gift away up to $22.8 million in assets before incurring federal estate or gift tax liabilities. However, once you reach the threshold, the estate and gift tax rate is 40%, although the estate and gift tax exemption is adjusted for inflation every year. Moreover, the generation-skipping transfer tax exemption has increased to $11.4 million per person, or $22.8 million for married couples. This is for gifts to grandchildren. Like before, once you are over the threshold, the tax rate is 40%, and adjusted yearly for inflation purposes.

8

OTHER DOCS

Power of Attorney. A Power of Attorney ("POA") is a very important legal document that can be used to appoint someone to conduct financial and legal decisions on behalf of someone else. There are two parties involved, the generator of the document (known as the principal) who is the one giving the right to another to act on their behalf, and the attorney-in-fact (known as the agent) who receives the right to act on the behalf of the principal. The POA has to be signed by the principal in the presence of two subscribing witnesses, and be notarized in order to be valid under Florida law. The Principal must be competent (sound mind) at the time of signing, and the attorney-in-fact must be at least 18 years old to serve as an agent. There are many things that the agent can do for the principal. For example, the agent can run the principal's business, manage bank accounts, and pay bills, loans, etc. This can apply to all of your financial affairs. e.g., paying loans, credit cards and other bills, signing contracts and deeds, and even filing your tax returns, among many other actions. Once you think about everything associated to your finances, you will get a clear picture for the purpose and importance of having this document in place. This document can be durable, which means that if you were to become incapacitated, your agent can continue to act on your behalf. A POA is effective until you pass away, revoke the document, or after any condition for its purpose is met.

Health Care Surrogate Designation. A Health Care Surrogate Designation (also known as a medical power of attorney) can be used to appoint someone to make medical decisions for you. This authority allows your agent to obtain your medical records and speak with your doctors about any information available to you. Moreover, if you are unable to speak with your doctor, specialist, or whomever, regarding a particular medical situation, your agent would step into your shoes and have these discussions in order to receive the information and make an informed decision on your behalf. This document is much broader than a Living Will.

Living Will. A Living Will is a written declaration by an adult (of sound mind) expressing their preferences to end-of-life medical treatment, specifically, the provision, the withholding or withdrawal of prolonging your life by administering procedures in the event of a terminal illness. The definition under the Florida law states "life prolonging procedures" includes any medical treatment or utilization of mechanical or artificial devices to sustain or replace a vital function, which is being used only to prolong the end of life stage of one who is terminally ill. This is an extremely important document because it alleviates the amount of stress the person who would have to make these decisions if this document was not previously executed by you, and you were unable to communicate with your doctor.

Preneed Guardian Designation. A Preneed Guardian Designation is a legal document that allows a parent, whether natural or adoptive, to designate someone to care for their minor child's well-being and their property. In Florida, if you are unable to care for your child due to incapacity, illness, or death, someone must become the child's legal guardian. However, the court will typically take your choice in consideration first, if you have previously designated a Guardian by executing a preneed guardian declaration. This applies to designating a preneed guardian for an adult as well.

Final Arrangements. A Final Arrangements Statement is a written document describing how to handle your final arrangements upon your passing. This letter will usually describe which funeral home to use, whether or not there will be a funeral service, a church service, and even if family members and friends are to gather at someone's home to mourn your passing with other family members. It can be as detailed as desired.

Letter of Intent. A Letter of Intent is simply a set of instructions made by the person creating a Last Will and Testament in order to assist their executor, beneficiaries, or even the judge in distributing their assets to their beneficiaries. It may also be used to clarify why certain property was given to certain individuals. However, it is important to know that this document is not legally binding or effective like a Last Will and Testament, but it can be used as an informal instrument to help guide and assist those individuals in charge of transferring property to their loved ones.

9

THE KIDS

Create the Plan. Florida law allows you to leave your children and your children's property to be cared for in several different ways.

Kids' Trust. As previously mentioned, the trust can be a valuable estate planning document, especially for your children. You can leave assets to your children and not have to worry about them misusing it or whether your children are adults, as the trust will instruct the trustee on how to use the trust's assets, which of course will be to the benefit of your children. Most trusts will state that the assets are to be used for your children's health, education, and well-being until the beneficiary receives the assets outright, which will be at the age you choose. However, if you do not create a trust or will, the probate court will designate a guardian of your children's property, until they reach 18 years old.

Guardian. As mentioned above, if you do not properly designate a guardian for your children upon your death, the probate court will do that for you considering the best interest of your child. However, a preneed guardian designation will address this matter, and the court will take your choice in consideration among other factors. Moreover, if you are unable to care for your minor child, and the need presented itself, the court would then have to appoint someone to care for your minor child, and again, the court will take your choice in consideration.

Designation of a Health Care Surrogate of a Minor. A Designation of a Health Care Surrogate of a Minor is a document that you execute that will avoid the need of going to court and appointing someone to make health care decisions for your child. You can also designate an alternate surrogate in case the primary surrogate is unable to perform for whatever reason. This document is very important, especially, if you are someone who is already receiving some type of medical treatment, and the possibility of requiring someone to make health care decisions for your child is great, or if you were to become incapacitated. Lastly, and equally important, included in this document is usually a HIPAA release, which allows your surrogate to receive medical records and confidential information that would otherwise be protected under the HIPAA statute.

Uniform Transfers to Minors Act. Florida law allows for the creation of custodial accounts for gifts to minors, however, according to this law, the age of a minor is anyone under the age of 21. The idea behind this account is very simple. Instead of creating a revocable trust, you can transfer your assets to an account controlled by a designated custodian, which must be for the benefit of a minor. The custodian can be a parent, grandparent, adult relative, or friend, etc. When the asset is transferred to the account, it now belongs to the minor, but managed by the custodian. This relationship creates a fiduciary duty where the custodian must act in the best interest of the minor. The asset can be of any nature i.e., stock, bonds, cash, mutual funds, intellectual property, life insurance, personal property, and title to real property. These accounts can be created simply by gift or by transfer from an estate or trust by the governing document, or by exercise of a power of appointment. Florida has now allowed custodianships to last until the beneficiary turns the age of 25. However, doing this is only possible if the minor is under the age of 21 at the time of your death. Moreover, a custodianship can be established if you, the custodian, or the minor resides in the state of Florida, or if the property is in Florida. Also, gifts via these accounts generally qualify for the gift tax exclusion under Section 2503(b) of the Code.

10

PROBATE

Probate. Refers essentially to the process of settling a decedent's debts and distributing his or her assets to their heirs. This, however, is a long and costly process. In Florida, a decedent's will must be submitted to the court within 10 days of their death, which is usually done by the attorney of the estate. Once the will is filed, the estate must be inventoried by the personal representative or executor. While the case is in probate, any outstanding debts or taxes are paid, heirs are notified, and any property is appraised, if necessary to determine their value. After all of this is done, the property is distributed to the rightful new owner. However, what if the deceased died without a will, or the will is contested, or the court determines that the will is invalid, the estate must still go through probate using the Florida's intestate succession statute. In either scenario, the probate process can take up to one year or more, which will depend on the complexity of the estate. This is one of the main reasons why people decide to use a living trust rather than relying solely on a will to determine how to distribute their assets upon death. Moreover, your designated personal representative or whoever the court has appointed is also entitled to reasonable fees.

Cost of Probate. As previously mentioned, the personal representative is entitled to collect fees from the estate for their part in administering the estate. If an attorney is hired by the personal representative, the attorney is entitled to fees. Furthermore, the court also charges fees for filing. So, with all of the potential fees, which are to be taken from the estate, you can quickly see how this can all add up. If someone fails to make an estate plan, then what's left to be distributed to heirs can literally be consumed from all of the fees.

11

THE VIEW FROM ABOVE

Why do any of this? Most of what we discussed in this book deals with planning what to do with your assets during your life and after your death. Your planning affects your loved ones, whether they are your children or your parents. Your planning affects your mental, emotional, spiritual, and physical well-being at the current stage of your life. Your planning will determine who is going to look after your children when you are not able to do so, and how they are to raise them. Your planning deals with your legacy, and how you will be remembered. Your planning will ultimately provide you peace of mind. Peace of mind that you have done for yourself all that could be planned while you were able to do so, and ensure that you were minimizing the amount of problems you were leaving behind for your family and friends to deal with when the time came.

CONCLUSION

It is in your best interest to consult with an attorney. The attorney will ultimately become an important part of your family's lives without a shadow of a doubt. I am speaking from experience, and know the value of building a long-lasting relationship with an attorney.

ABOUT THE AUTHOR

Gadiel A. Espinoza is a man of faith, father of two handsome young boys, husband to a beautiful and loving bride, son to a housekeeper and construction worker, brother to two strong women, friend to many, practicing attorney, and entrepreneur. He does not like to be labeled one particular thing as he believes labels are limitations that limit us from becoming our best. He lives in Miami, Florida with his wife and their two boys, and inspires to be a motivational speaker. He can be reached at GadielAEspinoza@Gmail.com, and/or followed on Instagram and fb.